COVENTRY SCHOOLS'
LIBRARY SERVICE

Please return this book on or before last
date stamped.

Viking Longboats

© Aladdin Books Ltd 2006

Designed and produced by
Aladdin Books Ltd
2/3 Fitzroy Mews
London W1T 6DF

Printed in Malaysia
All rights reserved

First published in 2006 by
Franklin Watts
338 Euston Road
London NW1 3BH

Franklin Watts Australia
Hachette Children's Books
Level 17/207 Kent Street
Sydney NSW 2000

A catalogue record for this book is available from the British Library

ISBN 0-7496-6823-7
ISBN 978-0-7496-6823-5
Dewey Classification: 948'.02

The **author**, Margaret Mulvihill, was born in Ireland and lives in London. She is the author of numerous articles for historical magazines and books as well as two novels and a biography.

Revised edition published in 2006
Original edition published as History Highlights – Viking Longboats
Design: David West Children's Book Design
Editor: Katie Harker
Picture researcher: Cecilia Weston-Baker
Illustrator: Tony Smith
Map: Alex Pang

Contents

Hallmarks of History

Viking Longboats

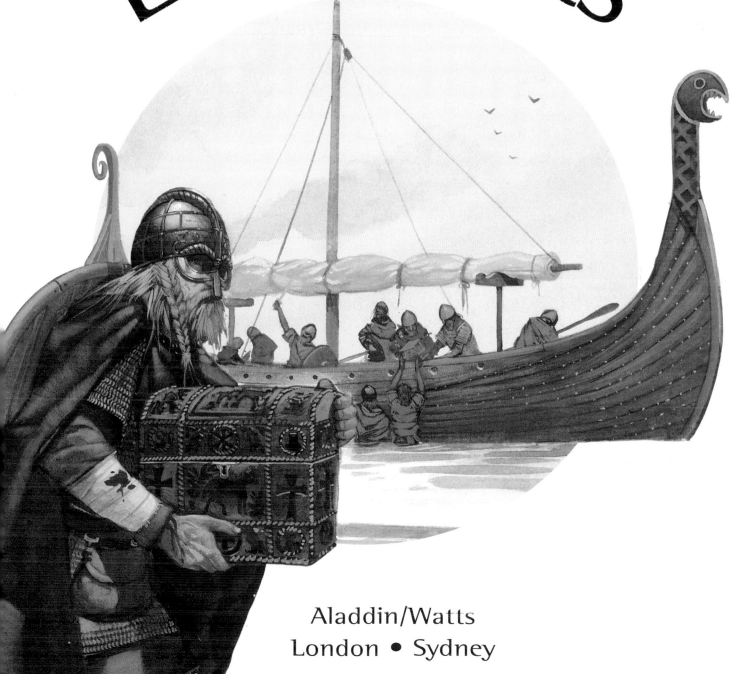

Aladdin/Watts

London • Sydney

Introduction

The Viking Age began in the late 8th century when people from Scandinavia travelled south to gain treasure and new land to settle on. Today, we know Scandinavia as the countries of Denmark, Norway and Sweden. The word 'viking' probably comes from 'vik' or 'vig', the Scandinavian word for 'creek' or 'battle'.

In the summer, these sailor-warriors crossed the seas in their wonderful ships. Their own countries had limitations – Norway was very mountainous, Sweden was covered in forests and Denmark had large areas of infertile land. So some of these Scandinavians settled in England, Scotland, Ireland, Germany, the Netherlands and France. Some also travelled through Russia, to the Arab world. The Viking Age lasted until about 1100.

Although their ships had sails, Vikings also rowed them. They used chests and barrels as seats. There was also room on board for animals and lots of cargo.

The Vikings

Norwegian, Swedish and Danish Vikings spoke different languages, but they could understand each other.

People thought the Vikings were unusually tall. The Germans called them ship-men, while the Arabs called them 'the heathen'.

Raiders from the sea

The Vikings were not Christians, and religious buildings were easy targets for their raids. In 793, Vikings attacked the island monastery of Lindisfarne, off the north-east coast of England. They destroyed this holy place, taking treasure and killing some of the monks, nuns and animals that lived there. The survivors were taken back to Scandinavia to become slaves. Similar Viking raids took place in Scotland, Ireland, Wales and on the continent of Europe.

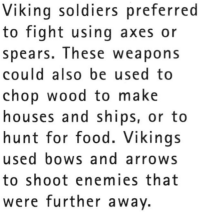

Viking soldiers preferred to fight using axes or spears. These weapons could also be used to chop wood to make houses and ships, or to hunt for food. Vikings used bows and arrows to shoot enemies that were further away.

In the 8th century, most of Europe was ruled by an emperor, called Charlemagne. When Charlemagne died in 814, however, his sons quarrelled over the empire. While they were busy fighting, large inland towns, such as Paris, were taken by the Vikings.

Viking warriors usually wore simple leather caps. Only the most important men wore armour, such as metal helmets and chain shirts. The Vikings took great pride in their weapons. The most important weapon was the sword. Families always passed special swords to younger generations.

Vikings learnt to build ships at an early age. They built them outside, as close to open water as possible. The wood from tall, straight oak trees was used to make the ship's keel (or bottom). The Vikings were the first people in northern Europe to build ships with sails. The ships had to be strong enough to carry the tall pine masts and sails.

Building longships

Viking ships were by far the best in Europe. They could sail very fast but they were also light enough to be carried.

Viking boats were called 'longships'. They were made with overlapping planks of wood that were nailed together. The joints were stuffed with ropes to make the boats watertight and flexible enough to sail in stormy seas. Vikings also used broader ships, called 'knorrs', for long journeys and for special fishing expeditions. We know how Viking boats were made because we have found the remains of some of these ships.

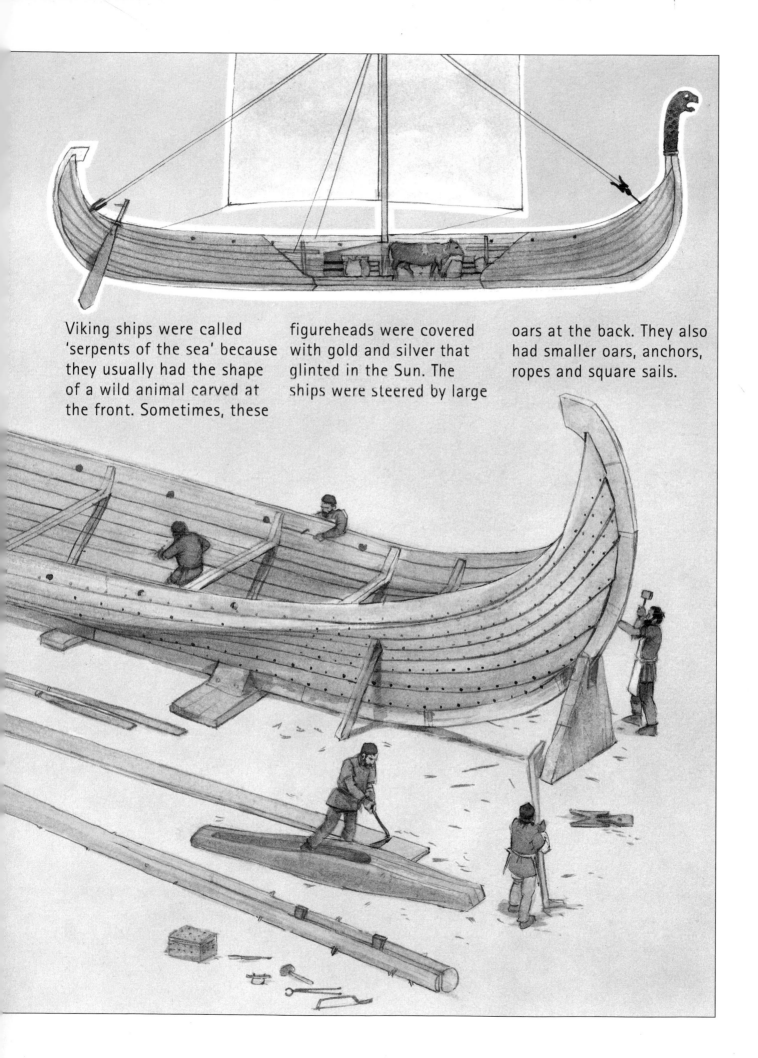

Viking ships were called 'serpents of the sea' because they usually had the shape of a wild animal carved at the front. Sometimes, these figureheads were covered with gold and silver that glinted in the Sun. The ships were steered by large oars at the back. They also had smaller oars, anchors, ropes and square sails.

Trade

As the Vikings travelled, they soon became important traders in Europe. They took goods from the north (such as furs, fish, wood, honey and whale oil) because they were valued in the south. In return, the Vikings brought back wines, spices, silk and silver from the south.

Swedish Vikings travelled through Russia to Byzantium (now Istanbul in Turkey). They were interested in valuable Arab silver coins and goods from the Far East, such as Chinese silk, oriental spices and Persian glass.

The Arabs were fascinated by the Vikings. They described them as being tall, with red faces and fearsome weapons. Viking men also loved to wear colourful clothes and precious jewellery. The Byzantine emperor was so impressed by these foreigners that he asked them to join his army.

Byzantium (now Istanbul) was a very civilised place in Viking times. Viking traders were impressed by the variety of goods offered by merchants there. The Vikings made a lot of money from their visits to Byzantium.

Travelling south

Swedish Vikings sailed along rivers in Russia. When they needed to travel overland, they used rollers to transport their ships. They used the Dnieper River and the Black Sea to reach Byzantium and the Volga River to reach the Caspian Sea.

The word Russia comes from 'rus', a Finnish word for Swedes. The Vikings set up the Russian cities of Novgorod and Kiev as places to trade. Other Vikings went west to England and France to get wheat, wool, tin, honey and salt.

ENGLAND Hedeby *Volga River*

Dnieper River

FRANCE Kiev

Black Sea Caspian Sea

Byzantium

Hedeby

Most Vikings were farmers who worked on the land. However, craftsmen, such as blacksmiths, weavers and carpenters, preferred to live in towns, where they could sell their goods. Viking towns were near to the sea. Hedeby in Denmark was a very large and successful Viking town. It was surrounded by thick, high walls made of earth and a strong sea wall made of wood. The merchants and craftsmen lived in wooden houses within these town walls.

Merchants came to Hedeby from around the world. They traded food, weapons and luxuries, such as furs and spices. Hedeby was also an important slave market. Prisoners of war were sold to the highest bidder as slaves (or 'thralls').

In 1050, Hedeby was raided and burned by the king of Norway. Many ships sank during the raid.

Archaeologists have used the town's remains to find out what daily life was like in a busy Viking town.

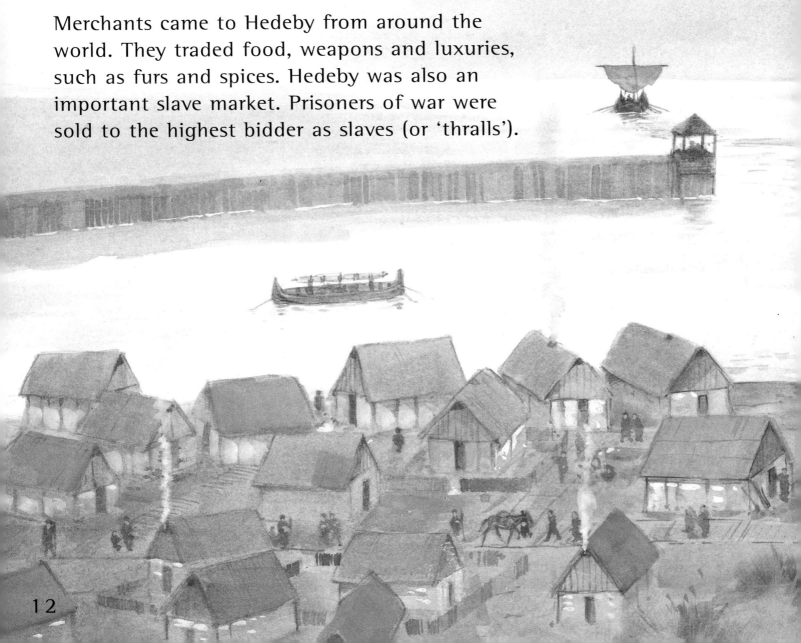

Viking silver

We have found many silver objects dating back to Viking times. In Sweden, for example, at least 40,000 Viking coins have been discovered. Silver was very valuable at the time. Rich Vikings hid their treasures and when they died, the silver was left behind.

Growing up

Viking children were taught to help adults. Girls were trained to run a household and to spin and weave cloth for clothes and ship sails. Boys learnt how to plough fields and to cut wood. They also helped with hunting, fishing and boat building.

Viking children played with model boats and wooden swords. They also liked to play ball games or board and dice games. In winter, ice-skating and skiing were popular activities.

Some Viking women were farmers and traders. When the Viking men went off travelling, other women were needed to help manage the farms. Viking marriages were arranged between families, but couples were allowed to separate.

A Viking house

The Vikings built their houses from wood or stone. The roofs were thatched with reeds or straw, or made from turf.

Viking families usually lived in one big room, where they would cook, eat, work and sleep. This room had a raised fireplace in the middle.

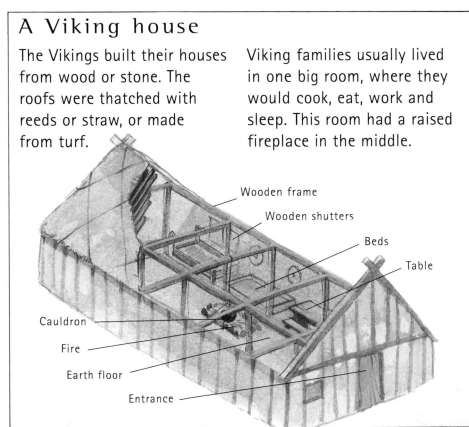

Wooden frame
Wooden shutters
Beds
Table
Cauldron
Fire
Earth floor
Entrance

A woman in charge of a household wore her keys on a chain dangling from a brooch near her shoulder. This was to show her authority. Viking houses were warm but they smelt of smoke because the roof only had a small hole to let out smoke from the fire. Other buildings near to a Viking home were used as stables, barns, toilets or workshops for weaving and metal work.

Farming and fishing

The Vikings made almost everything they needed. They grew crops of rye, barley, wheat and oats to make their daily meals. Vegetables, such as peas and beans, were grown near to the house and nuts and other vegetables were gathered from the wild.

The Vikings went hunting and fishing all year round. They used fishing lines, traps and nets to catch fish in streams, lakes and the sea. The fish were dried on racks and then salted or smoked. Large sea mammals, such as seals, walruses and whales, were also hunted.

In summer, the Vikings kept sheep and cows in their fields. As winter approached, some of these animals were killed. The meat was salted or pickled to preserve it. Vikings got their salt by boiling seawater. The meat was then roasted on a spit, stewed in a cauldron or cooked next to hot stones.

The whole family worked on the farm. They were helped by thralls (slaves) or karls (men who did not own any land). There was plenty of work to do. Food was stored in larders for the long winter. The Vikings also buried butter in tubs in the ground and hung dried fish and meat on the outside walls of their homes.

Bone and antler

The Vikings made many things from the bones and antlers of the animals they hunted. The antlers from deer were used to make combs (top left). Bone was used to make pins and needles (centre right) and tools for spinning wool (the circular and longer objects in this picture). Pieces of Viking material can also be seen (top right).

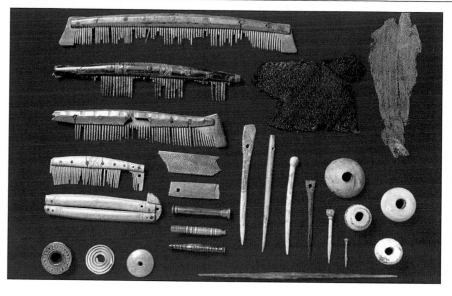

Feasting

The Vikings looked forward to their feasts. During these holidays, families came together and exchanged news and ideas. Weddings and other deals were also arranged.

There were three major feasts in the year – one after the shortest day of winter, one in April and another in October to celebrate the harvest. Before a celebration, sacrifices were offered to the gods. In April, the gods would be asked for victory in the battles and raids to come. All the guests gathered in their finest clothes, to eat and drink in a big hall. Spectator sports were also often held outside.

The special meat eaten at a Viking feast was horsemeat. The Vikings also drank beer, mead and wine (if they were wealthy). Cattle horns were used as cups. Feasts were usually accompanied by entertainment, such as poetry recitals and music.

Runes

The borders of this chest were decorated with runes – the Viking alphabet of letters made up of straight lines. Runes were easy to carve on wood, bone and even stone.

Vikings carved their names on personal things such as combs and gravestones, and on landmarks of the places they visited. There were only 16 letters in the runic alphabet.

Religion

The Vikings worshipped their gods outside, near to natural landmarks such as huge rocks, unusual trees or waterfalls. They believed in life after death and thought that people would need material things in the next world. Ordinary women were buried with food, clothes and a cooking pot. Wealthy people were buried with their whole 'ship' household. Some slaves were even killed to accompany their owners to heaven.

The Vikings thought that if you died in battle you went to a special heaven. The chief Viking god, Odin, was said to send warrior maidens called 'Valkyries' to take soldiers to a great hall known as Valhalla. Here, they would spend the rest of their days feasting and drinking. With the thought of Valhalla as their reward, Viking soldiers showed great courage.

In 1903, the remains of a Viking ship were discovered in Norway. The Oseberg ship was probably built in 800 and buried in 850. It contained the skeletons of two women, one of whom may have been a princess or a queen. The ship was also full of valuable goods and the skeletons of at least ten horses and two oxen.

Viking gods

This tapestry shows three Viking gods – Odin (with axe), Thor (with hammer) and Frey (with corn). Odin was the chief god. He was very wise and knew about magic and the dead. Thor was the mother goddess Frigg's son, and made the noise of thunder with his great hammer. Frey was the god in charge of all growing things and of peace and plenty.

It was said that Frigg spun gold thread on her spinning wheel and wove it into summer clouds. In exchange for sacrifices made at Viking feasts, the gods were supposed to give good winters, harvests and victories in battles.

Government

The more land and money a Viking had, the more important his family was. Sometimes, arguments between families lasted for generations. If a family member was murdered, this brutal act had to be punished. A relative would take revenge by killing the murderer.

Some arguments were settled at an open air meeting instead. All the freemen in the district met regularly to discuss problems and to settle arguments about money, thefts, divorce, murder and the ownership of land. These meetings were called 'Things'.

In Iceland, a Viking meeting (called an Althing) took place every summer at the Thingvellir, a large area in front of a lava cliff. Sometimes, quarrels were settled by duels to the death.

Every man who owned property could vote, but the wealthier you were, the more influence you had. Large national Things met each summer and could last for weeks. At these great social events, news was exchanged and business arrangements were made.

Most crimes were punished by banishment or a fine. Erik the Red, for example, was banished from Norway. When he murdered a man in Iceland he was banished again. A banished man could be lawfully killed if he did not leave.

Some Things tried to settle matters in other ways. In Iceland, women were asked to pick stones from a pot of boiling water. If their wounds healed, the Vikings thought they were telling the truth.

Vinland

Around 860, a severe storm blew a Swedish viking ship to the coast of Iceland. The island became colonised and by 930 about 50,000 people were living there.

When Erik the Red was banished from Iceland in 982, he sailed westwards and discovered another large island. The island was cold with little farming land, but to encourage people to settle, he gave the island a pleasant name – Greenland. Eventually about 3,000 people settled there. They began hunting whales for their food.

Erik the Red's son, Leif Erikson, discovered a place he called Vinland (now part of North America). Leif stayed in Greenland, but with its fertile land, others thought that Vinland was an ideal place to settle.

Life in Vinland was easier than in Greenland. The good weather meant that cattle could survive outside all year round. At first the settlers got on very well with the North American Indians, who traded with them. But after a few years the settlers and the Indians became enemies. The Vinlanders were forced to sail away, and Vinland never grew into a permanent colony.

For a long time people were not sure whether the story of Vinland was a myth or a true story, but in 1961 archaeologists found the remains of a Viking settlement at L'Anse-aux-Meadows in Newfoundland, an island off the east coast of Canada.

Although the American Indians were frightened of the Vinlanders' animals, they enjoyed the taste of the milk from the settlers' cattle. The Indians also liked the red cloth the Vikings brought from Greenland. They exchanged skins and furs for some of this cloth.

What happened?

After about 1066, the Vikings began to lead more settled lives as townsmen and farmers and life became more peaceful. The Vikings also became Christians and trading soon took over from their raiding.

Around this time, it also became harder to raid other countries which had formed strong armies to resist attacks. The king of France, for example, gave the shores of northern France to a Danish chief called Rollo. Rollo defended the area (which was later called Normandy) from other Vikings. Once Rollo's followers married into the local communities, it was difficult to tell the difference between the Vikings and the locals.

In 1066, William, the Duke of Normandy, landed in southern England. His armies defeated the English king and William and his followers seized English lands. William was descended from the Viking chief, Rollo, who had married a local Frenchwoman. William was so well settled in France that he and his followers were called 'Normans'.

The Bayeux Tapestry

This part of the Bayeux Tapestry shows a Norman fleet invading England. The tapestry was made by Norman women in the 11th century to commemorate the Norman invasion of England. It is now kept in Bayeux in northern France.

Viking traces

We know about life during the Viking Age from the coins, weapons, jewellery and other remains we have discovered. Many Viking influences can also be found in our languages. The word Thursday comes from 'Thor's Day', for example. Many English words to do with trading and sailing also have Viking origins.

The Vikings gave us other things, too. Our modern-day parliaments, for example, developed from Viking assemblies (Things). Many of today's important towns and cities originate from Viking settlements. The Vikings often lived near to the sea or by rivers because these places were good trading routes.

These fishermen are working off the Scottish coast. Vikings settled in the nearby islands of Orkney and Shetland, in the 9th century. The islands still have many Viking customs.

Up Hellya

At the end of January, some people in the Shetland Islands celebrate a festival called the 'Up Hellya'. After a torchlit procession they set fire to a longboat. For this feast and celebration most people wear fancy dress. Some people actually dress up as Vikings.

Date charts

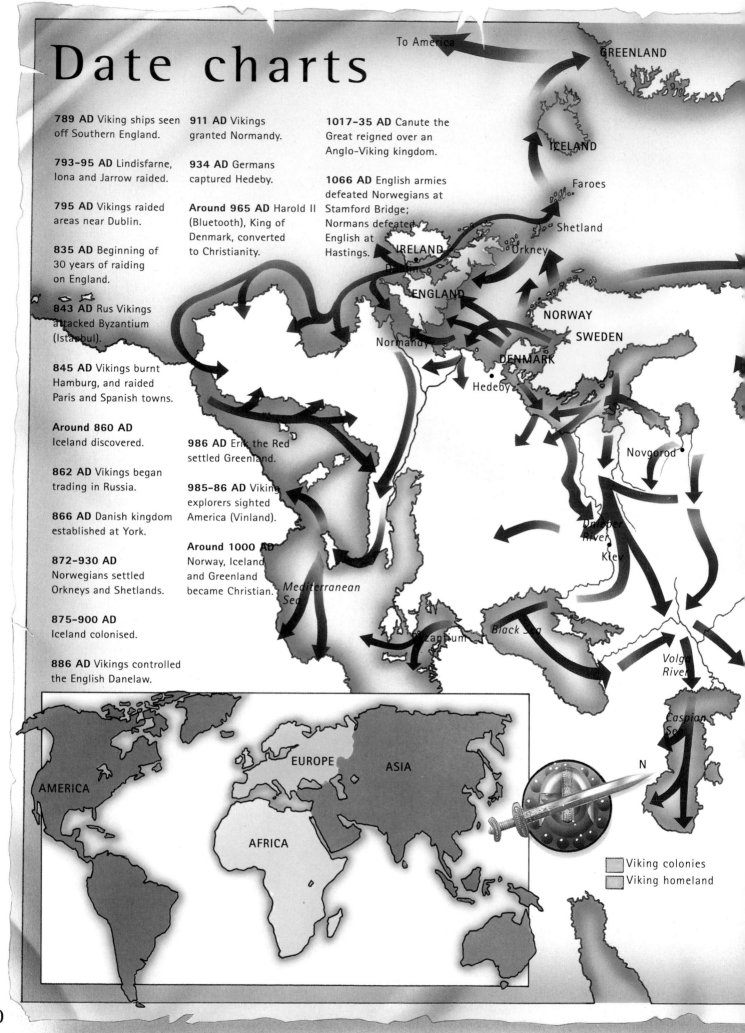

789 AD Viking ships seen off Southern England.

793–95 AD Lindisfarne, Iona and Jarrow raided.

795 AD Vikings raided areas near Dublin.

835 AD Beginning of 30 years of raiding on England.

843 AD Rus Vikings attacked Byzantium (Istanbul).

845 AD Vikings burnt Hamburg, and raided Paris and Spanish towns.

Around 860 AD Iceland discovered.

862 AD Vikings began trading in Russia.

866 AD Danish kingdom established at York.

872–930 AD Norwegians settled Orkneys and Shetlands.

875–900 AD Iceland colonised.

886 AD Vikings controlled the English Danelaw.

911 AD Vikings granted Normandy.

934 AD Germans captured Hedeby.

Around 965 AD Harold II (Bluetooth), King of Denmark, converted to Christianity.

986 AD Erik the Red settled Greenland.

985–86 AD Viking explorers sighted America (Vinland).

Around 1000 AD Norway, Iceland and Greenland became Christian.

1017–35 AD Canute the Great reigned over an Anglo-Viking kingdom.

1066 AD English armies defeated Norwegians at Stamford Bridge; Normans defeated English at Hastings.

To America

GREENLAND

ICELAND

Faroes

Shetland

Orkney

IRELAND

Dublin

ENGLAND

NORWAY

SWEDEN

Normandy

DENMARK

Hedeby

Novgorod

Dnieper River

Kiev

Mediterranean Sea

Byzantium

Black Sea

Volga River

Caspian Sea

N

EUROPE

ASIA

AMERICA

AFRICA

Viking colonies
Viking homeland

Africa	Asia	Americas	Europe
641 AD Arabs took over Egypt and overran North Africa.	**618 AD** T'ang Dynasty in China established.	**600 AD onwards** Late Classic period of the Mayan Empire.	**711 AD** Arabs conquered Spain, except the Asturias.
700 AD Arab traders set up trading settlements in East Africa. Coptic Christians in Ethiopia.		**650–900 AD** Huastecan culture on Gulf coast of Mexico.	**732 AD** Battle of Poitiers: the Arabs were defeated in southern France.
	751 AD Arabs defeated Chinese in central Asia.	**750 AD** Mayan Empire declined.	**790s AD** Viking raids began.
800 AD Beginning of Kanem Empire in central Sudan.			**800 AD** Charlemagne crowned.
			840s AD Dublin founded.
850 AD The city of Great Zimbabwe built.			**851 AD** Danish army wintered in England.
			860s AD Swedish Vikings active in Russia; Vikings took over York.
			871–99 AD Reign of Alfred the Great over Wessex (West of England).
920–1050 AD Height of the empire of Ghana, West Africa.	**907 AD** End of the T'ang Dynasty in China.	**900 AD** Beginning of Mixtec culture in Mexico.	**911 AD** Rollo granted Normandy.
969 AD Fatamids conquered Egypt and found Cairo.	**960 AD** Sung Dynasty re-united China.	**980 AD** Toltec capital set up at Tula (Mexico).	
1000s AD Beginning of the Yoruba Empire on the Niger.	**Around 1000 AD** Gunpowder invented in China.	**1000 AD** Leif Erikson travelled down the American coast.	**Around 1000 AD** Iceland became Christian.
	1037 AD Seljuk Turks invaded Khorasian, Jurjan and Tabaristan.		**1017–35 AD** Reign of King Canute.
1054 AD Ghana conquered by the Almoravid Berbers from the north.	**1055 AD** Tughril Beg entered Baghdad and was proclaimed sultan.		**1066 AD** English defeated Norwegians at Stamford Bridge; Normans defeated English at Hastings.
	1071 AD Seljuks defeated Byzantines.		**1079–81 AD** El Cid campaigned against Moorish kingdom of Toledo in Spain.
			1080 AD King of Norway converted to Christianity.
			1096 AD The First Crusade.

Index

Photographic credits:
The publisher would like to thank the Jorvik Centre/York Archaeological Trust for providing illustrative reference material for this book. Back cover, 12, 18 – Michael Holford. 17 – The York Archaeological Trust. 21 – Werner Forman Archive. 27 – Mary Evans Picture Library. 29 – David Simson/ Shetland Tourist Organisation.